I0483066

Dedication:
Volume 1 Arianna Warner's Family

The Dedication Project

Visit The Dedication Project website at: www.dedicationproject.com.

First Printing June 2014.
Createspace: An Amazon Company

Title ID: 4701945
ISBN-13: 978-1496154835

1

Dedication:

Volume 1 Arianna Warner's Family

The Dedication Project

Authors:
Mindie Galgoul || Ian Maile || Bob Warner || Barbara Ayala || Evangeline Dominguez || Craig Jimenez || Debbie Ayala || Hank Lopez || Frances Warner || Sue Naylor Clark || Gloria (Cookie) Gomez || Zachary Ayala || Gaby Fisher || Abby Warner || Mary Prieto || Kimberly Ayala Warner || Sheetal Prieto || Stacey Medina || Adie Maile || Chris Warner || Brianna Galgoul || Michael Prieto || Kenny Ayala || Dana Ayala || Kerri Hogan || Dave Warner || Robyn Robinson || Becky Ayala || Jesse Ayala || Katie Ingram || Arianna Warner

Created by: Arianna Warner

For my grandmother, Anna Vold Naylor.

She, by example, taught me about strength, independence, and family. As a teenager you immigrated from Norway alone on a "sailing ship"; whether whim or necessity drove that choice no one ever may know. Widowed and left with two small boys to rear alone, you took in strangers' laundry and worked menial jobs through lean Depression years, somehow emerging an esteemed pastry chef and jet-setting between northern and southern hotels every summer and winter, long before most ever dreamed of, much less realized, such a lifestyle . . . for a woman! You learned English by studying the newspaper, and wrote to the girl I was, remembered every birthday and Christmas, sent gifts for no reason, and never said a word against the daughter-in-law, my mother, who, I later learned, scorned and shunned you for your modest origins. They didn't tell me when you passed; I had no chance to say good-bye. It's just as well, for you live every day in my heart and in any good I do. I am grateful.

For my father, Antonio Jose Prieto a.k.a. "Viejo".

As his third and youngest daughter, I was well positioned to be led, guided, and loved by this amazing man who mastered the art of fatherhood. In other words, I was not his first rodeo... any kinks there might have been with his first child were long gone when I arrived.

What do you say about a man who embodied the meaning of the word father? That he was loving, honest, fair, fun, generous, strong, kind? Yes, my Viejo was all those things... and more. He ALWAYS, ALWAYS put his children first. All he did was in his children's best interest. He taught us to love God fiercely, love each other unconditionally, learn all that we could, work hard, give to others, and to leave the world a better place than when we were born. He taught us that the world would be challenging and hard and unfair but that we had God on our side so we could overcome anything and we could keep moving forward... we have... and we do. Thanks, Viejo.

For my mother, Lupe Lopez Prieto.

Mom, thank you for loving and caring so deeply for your family. You were so beautiful and always smiling, singing, and laughing. There are so many wonderful memories of you that will forever remain in my heart. You always put your children and Dad first and sacrificed your own needs and dreams. Getting a good education was so important to you, and you also had me take tap, ballet, piano, and accordion lessons.

There were dreams that were never fulfilled in your youth but you saw to it that I would have opportunities to learn all that life had to offer. You were so proud and happy with everything I did, and each one of your children had a special place in your heart.

All of my life you showed me courage, strength, faith, and love especially with Dad and Chuckie's deaths and your own struggle with cancer. You have always inspired me by your example on how to live life. Because of you, I am a better person.

You were the "Wind Beneath My Wings".

For my dad, Leonard Ayala.

Leonard was the sixth of nine siblings. After graduating high school, he took on many jobs so that he could help out his family financially. He served his country in the Army, then married my mom, Josephine. Soon after he began a career as a carpenter. He is a proud man and devoted, loving father. From a young age, I recall my dad coming home from work exhausted. He encouraged me to always do well in school and to never stop going to school. Education was important to him as he wanted all of his children to have a great education and a better opportunity than he did. We all attended private school. As a teenager I remember sitting with my dad in the kitchen and him telling me to look at his hands (they were swollen and calloused). He told me, "Son, go to college and promise me that you will not get involved in construction." Because of his encouraging words and support, I graduated from college, work as a professional, and continue my education.

For my sister, Gaby Galgoul.

Even though she is my younger sister, she is wise beyond her years. This person has stood by me and judged me, when needed. Being a strong, beautiful, intelligent, veterinarian, wife, mother, sister, and friend, she maintains her dignity and grace with ease. She has accomplished so much in her 30 years and has created the most beautiful family. I have learned strength and growth through our sisterhood. I hope I can always be as honest, opinionated, and confident. Thank you sister for always being someone I can count on whenever. I can't wait for you to stand beside me at my wedding.

For my mother, Jessie Frizzelle.

She was a very strong person and instilled in me strong values. She always encouraged me to reach high and try harder to better myself. She encouraged me to stay in school when I wanted to quit school after the 8th grade, like some of my friends were doing. When her talks did not work, she turned to bribery with things I really wanted, such as Cashmere Sweaters, a watch, etc., which worked. Again I wanted to quit school after the 10th grade and again she used bribery to keep me in school. This time it was a used car, which I wanted enough to stay in school. After graduating from high school, I thought this is enough school and again she bribed me with a New car if I graduated with my Associates degree. She always believed and instilled in me the importance of an education and of course she was right. I believe now my life would have been very different had I not stayed in school. My mom was my hero.

For my dad, Kenny Ayala.

I don't know where you learn how to be a dad; but my dad is great. He inspires me every day. He is young enough to play with me and old enough to be a good example. We always joke around, and he is fun to be around. He shows me how to be a good person. He has coached my soccer, lacrosse, and basketball teams; he is there for all of my activities. He shares my school experiences with me. Last year he chaperoned my field trip to Sacramento. Like any good mentor, he tells me how to be better. We have a lot in common, for example sports, cars, pets, and travel. Each year our family vacation is based on my interests- my parents don't go on vacation without me. He tells me that he wants to share time with me. My dad has had a huge impact on my life. I know he tries to do all he can for me. He puts himself second for me and says what's his is mine. Everyone should have a dad like mine generous, intelligent, and dedicated.

For my father-in-law, Grandpa Tony (Antonio Prieto).

He influenced me with respect, love, and the support of family. No judgments. He truly believed in supporting all family no matter who they were and what they were going through. Grandpa used to tell me our kids are grown in the blink of an eye and now I can see what he meant. I feel blessed that my boys had the time they did with their grandpa. He was always there for them and tried to teach them to always support one another. I wish he could have stayed with us just a little longer. Hopefully, we will all be reunited again.

For the two loves of my life,
Raegan Marie and Grant Lopez.

They are my sunshine and make me happy
when skies are gray. I hope you always know (both of
you) my love for you is way, way, more than you
will ever know.

For my DAD, Roland Perez Ayala.

He meant the world to me. I was the apple of his eye and we shared that special father daughter bond. He was the most patient, loving, and caring father. His unconditional love inspires me and how giving he was of his time, like when he took me out of school to spend the day with him. His love for life was contagious: always dancing, and partying. He loved deeply caring for others, including his children and *compadres*. He would drop things at a moment's notice to help me. I love you, Dad!

For my wife, Rhonda Marie (White) Lopez.

She is my inspiration and what gives meaning to my life. She has remained constant in my life for over 40 years. From the first time I laid eyes on her I wanted to get to know her. It sounds crazy but she was wearing a shorts outfit with knee socks; it was awesome. She has always stood behind me in simple and hard decisions I (we) have made over the years. She is the calm when things get wild, she is the wind in my sail, and most importantly she is the love of my life. She is a beautiful person inside and out, a wonderful wife, mother, and now grandmother.

For my older sister, Brianna Rose Galgoul.

When we were younger I used to look up to you because you were always surrounded by friends and had a positive and fun outlook on life. Now as adults I look up to you because of your amazing spirit and ability to dance through life with your beautiful smile no matter the challenge. You have grown into an amazing woman, teaching me to relax and try to enjoy life a little more. You are an amazing support system, and I am so incredibly lucky to have you as my big sister. You have been especially important to me during the birth and life of my son. You are a wonderful and positive light in Jacob's life; because of you he will truly understand what it means to live each day to the fullest. Your smile and positive energy is contagious, and when I see you or talk to you I always find myself smiling and in a happy mood. Thank you for teaching me how to find happiness in any situation and inspiring me to dance a little more.

For my step-mother, Hazel Klug.

She came into my life at the age of three. My father needed someone to assist him in caring for me and Hazel married my father in 1932. My mother taught high school Spanish. When I was seven years old and bedridden, my mother would bring me bags of books from the library for me to read. This has contributed to my lifelong love of reading. While looking for posters to decorate her classroom, my mother saw beautiful posters of the Mexican countryside, Mexican culture, and the Mexican railroad. She purchased a few posters and met a Mexican woman who would later care for me. My mother developed a love for the Mexican culture and my mother and I travelled to Mexico at the end of World War II. I have shared this love of Mexico with my husband and sons, and I have enjoyed travelling to Mexico throughout my life.

For my grandpa, Tony Preito.

Growing up, I can recall having many one-on-one talks about life with him. He would be honest about any questions I would ask and tell great stories of my mom growing up. Grandpa Tony was looked upon as the head of our family and had a physical presence in the room. He was loved by so many, but most important his immediate family. He would cook for the family and provide so much more for all. I looked up to him for his strong mentality on life. Anytime a family member was ill, he would say, "kick that old misery"! He would flex his muscular forearms and make a tattoo of a woman in a bikini shake. He got it while in the military, where he was described as a tough guy. When he past away, I cried so much because he was my favorite and missed him greatly. I respect him so much that I know a big part of my life and attitudes of how I live it is because of him. Grandpa Tony Preito spirit is alive in all our hearts!

For my mother, Tila Lopez Leal.

She was always the one person who I looked up to. What a wonderful beautiful person she was; strong, generous to all when they needed help. She was very intelligent, wise in her integrity to her behaviors (believes) in her Godlyhood never wavered.

She worked hard from a young woman to her old age (89 years) in selling avon for her children and family- near a perfect person.

May God keep her in his memory.

For Harold Klug.

He taught me perseverance and the importance of my inner child. Despite being told he shouldn't bother with high school, this blacksmith's son graduated from high school, college, became a teacher, the superintendent of the school district, and a lawyer. He believed in self-reliance and didn't shy away from hard work. He loved his family and when his young bride died in 1929, he faced the challenge of raising an infant and the great depression head on. He raised rabbits and chickens for meat and eggs in the backyard to raise a little money. Despite the harsh realities, he always believed it was important to create, discover and marvel at things throughout his life. He taught his daughter this and she passed it on to me. As a boy, I remember looking above his desk and seeing a troll doll. It was a child's toy, but it was clearly important to him. Harold passed away years ago, but I have his troll and think of what he went through, what he valued and what he passed on to me.

For my beautiful wife.

Thank you for adding so much value to my life experiences. You highlight every day with a smile and enrich everything I do to help maximize this journey. Your love is the greatest impact.

For my mom, Josephine Ayala.

She has truly made a positive impact in my life. I think as a child, you really don't realize what your parents mean to you until you become a parent yourself. The bright light goes on and, 'boom!' You appreciate now, the times you were disciplined. And it makes you a better person and parent. If I am in a certain dilemma with my own children, I would ask myself, "how would Mom handle this?" My mom taught me to always have compassion for those who are less fortunate, to love my brothers with all my heart, and to respect and acknowledge those around you. I instill these precious qualities in my children. When I see them act upon it, I smile and think of my mom. I am forever grateful to my mom. Love you, Mom!

For my sister, Alexandra Warner.

The first day I walked into my life I knew my sister would be by my side. Alex taught me the importance of dedication, by showing me the means and motivation. Sophomore year in High School I was not doing so hot in chemistry class, so Alex decided to help me pass the class. Every Friday for the entire semester she tutored me during lunch in the library. She encouraged me to work hard and study. At the end of the semester I got an A. That is when I realized that she helps me way more than I acknowledge by teaching me all these small lessons that morph me into a better person.

For my mom, Alice Medina.

The first thing that comes to mind is- "Where is your sweater?" She is always worried about someone being cold. She is insistent on always carrying a sweater "just in case", even if it's in the middle of summer. Alice has given away hundreds of sweaters. She has made it her responsibility to keep everyone warm.

My mom was the cook, chauffeur, plumber, housekeeper, tutor, gardener, bookkeeper, and mother; she did an excellent job at each and never complained.

She loved having family and friend gatherings, welcoming all into our home. She would cook and cook and cook, and we would all eat and eat and eat. She also opened our door to kids having difficult times at home. She fed them, listened to them, and gave them a place to sleep. To this day, she is still visited by the grateful people she took in. She is one of the many great women in my life. She taught me to be compassionate and kind, and not to judge. My door is always open to anyone who needs a good meal, an ear to listen, or a warm sweater.

For my grandmother.

She was a woman who embodied the word family. Whether it was through hauling her grand-kids on a train to head downtown for an adventure or making our favorite foods for breakfast, the love she shone on us was raw, wholehearted and amazingly sweet. My love for family comes from the examples she set for me while interacting with others. Never putting herself first, if her family was happy, she was happy. So simple, so pure. The selflessness she demonstrated on a daily basis was prevalent even towards the end of her life when she became ill. Having been in the presence of her giving and loving spirit inspires me to do better, be kinder, and love deeper.

For the black sheep of my family,
and to those that try to include us.

At times in my relationship with my family / I feel I don't fit in. / It has happened for myriad reasons; / a person, a place, an idea, belief or perception, / an activity, an event, sometimes a memory. / It becomes difficult, if not impossible, to join in, / to feel any sense of belonging. / To those that are reading this and have felt that / Insecurity, that uncertainty and that struggle to participate / to go, to try to be a part of. / To the black sheep of my family...

And there are individuals, situations, occasions / where in spite of my ill-temper, members of my family / have reached out, have tried to hold the space / I have needed to be. / In this way they show they have cared for me. / Not all black sheep are so lucky to have people in their family / that try to create connection, to draw them in, / to make you a part of, to create belonging. / It must be tremendously difficult to do / But your efforts are not in vain / To those that try to include us black sheep.

For my Pop-Pop, Leonard Ayala.

He served in the United States Army. He doesn't struggle with his hearing even though he wears a hearing -aid. He loves everyone. He's caring. He's funny and makes me laugh all the time. He has a injured knee, but that does not stop him. He still walks as much as he can. My Pop-Pop is the best. I love you Pop-Pop!!!

For my dad, Robert Carrillo.

He was 20 when he married my mom, worked full time and took night courses at a community college. I remember most nights he swooped in as we sat down for dinner, grabbed his books and left while we were still eating. I recall hearing the sound of the typewriter late at night as he completed papers.

When I was in elementary school he transferred to a university. I was 8 when I realized that not everyone's dad went to college at night. When I questioned my dad about this, he told me that he wanted to be the best example for us. He attended every performance, and awards assembly for me and coached my brothers' baseball teams. When I was in high school, he was in Law School, still working full time. He graduated and passed the California Bar as I attended college.

Now, as a parent, I see how difficult it would be to attend class or study at night after a long day at work. His encouragement and resolve for education motivated me through college and graduate school.

For Bob.

For being my brother despite his introduction of harpoons to our brood.

In my first year of college he and his good friend Steve Crump came to visit. While I spent little time with them (instead choosing a fleeting romance with a girl), my behavior didn't harm our relationship one bit.

After Bob later married, he and his life partner, Kim, welcomed my family into their lives, repeatedly sharing experiences of how rich life is: Our kids playing in the waves at the beach for hours. Hanging out at the pool eating snacks. Or tolerating a brother who brings a bag of squirt guns to a birthday dinner.

Months or more have gone by where we haven't spoken. Whenever we did next speak it would be as if no time had passed at all.

Perhaps he has known it all along, but as I get older I realize it is more important to not let time go by like that as we won't always be around. But Bob's okay with me either way.

For my grandmother, Gloria Ayala.

As a middle age woman, oldest grandchild in the family, I have the upmost respect for my grandmother. She is 85 years old and loves to tell stories. I've come to realize the true meaning of just listening to your elders. There will be no eyes rolling with me when I am conversing with my grandmother. Her stories and memories mean so much to me; especially since I lost my father, Ralph Ayala Jr. her oldest son, 20 years ago. I will always cherish, respect, love, and savor what she has to offer, not only me, but my three children- Deja, Demi, and Devon Ayala.

For Geraldine, my MOM.

As my eyes well up and tears fall all I can do is thank you for being the AMAZING WOMAN that you were... My mom, Geraldine, or Gerri as she liked to be called was the most amazing woman I have ever met. My mom, Geraldine, showed me by way of example how amazing she was; never turned her back on family or friends. My mom, Geraldine, showed me by way of example to love everyone to not pass judgment on others as you never knew what was truly in their hearts. My mom, Geraldine, showed me by way of example how to be a compassionate person - through charity work, feeding the homeless man in our neighborhood, helping those in need no matter what their situation was; being a loving person a forgiving person a hard working person and best of all, a mom. My mom, Geraldine, was and will always be the most amazing woman I know, and I hope to be at least half as amazing as she was. MOM this is dedicated to YOU the most AMAZING WOMAN I KNOW.

For my mother, Lorraine Ayala.

My mom has always been a positive person in my life, she had more strength than anyone I know. My mother was married to my dad at only 16 years of age, and is still married to my dad, after 52 years. My mother taught me how to love unconditionally, how to forgive, and that a mother never gives up on her children. Holidays and birthday were always fantastic full of love and fun for all. During the low parts of my life, my mom was there for me, as well as being there to share my happiest moments; my mother is an amazing woman. I hope I can be even half the woman she is. I love my mom more than words can say! Thank you mom for being the best mother ever.

For my grandfather (Christy) Alfredo Ayala.

He has been in my life since birth. He has always shown me so much love and any attention. I did not grow up knowing my father, but my grandfather made sure I never felt alone or left out. He took me hunting, fishing, and taught me so many things my mom just couldn't. He inspires me to always do my best and I want to make him proud. He came from very modest means, was the youngest of nine, and over came so many things in his life. He only made it to the 6th grade, yet he was able to have a very successful life. He raised three children who wanted for nothing, and was always loving and respectful to my grandma. He's funny and silly too. He's the best. I still love spending time with him.

For Justin Cullpepper.

Justin Cullpepper impacted my life in so many ways. He was a high school friend of my Aunt Kristina Ayala, and he rented a room from my mom; instantly Justin became family. He was so nice and always trying to help around the house from chores, to listening to my mom, sister, brother, and me. I was very close to Justin. He never judged people, yet he was constantly being judged for his sexuality. He was the kindest person I've ever met and when we lost him, I was devastated. There is not a day that goes by that he is not on my mind. He died at only 24 years old, from suicide. I know he's with the angels in heaven and is finally at peace. I will never forget my wonderful friend and the happiness he brought to my life.

For Grandpa Roland.

For always pushing me, inspiring me, and loving me. You will forever be with me, and I will always hear you on the sidelines yelling, "Do it for Grandpa!".

Dedication Index

Hank Lopez- *For my wife, Rhonda Marie (White) Lopez 21*

Gaby Galgoul- *For my older sister, Brianna Rose Galgoul 23*

Frances Warner- *For my step-mother, Hazel Klug 25*

Craig Jimenez- *For my grandpa, Tony Preito 27*

Evangeline Dominguez- *For my mother, Tila Lopez Leal 29*

Bob Warner- *For Harold Klug 31*

Michael Prieto- *For my beautiful wife 33*

Adie Maile- *For my mom, Josephine Ayala 35*

Abby Warner- *For my sister, Alexandra Warner 37*

Stacey Medina- *For my mom, Alice Medina 39*

Sheetal Prieto- *For my grandmother 41*

Chris Warner- *For the black sheep of my family, and those that try to include us 43*

Ian Maile- *For my Pop-Pop, Leonard Ayala 45*

Debbie Ayala- *For my dad, Robert Carrillo 47*

Dave Warner- *For Bob 49*

Dana Ayala- *For my grandmother, Gloria Ayala 51*

Robyn Robinson- *For Geraldine, my MOM 53*

Becky Ayala- *For my mother, Lorraine Ayala 55*

Jesse Ayala- *For my grandfather (Christy) Alfredo Ayala 57*

Katie Ingram- *For Justin Culpepper 59*

Arianna Warner- *For Grandpa Roland 61*

Acknowledgments

Special thanks to my wonderful family for participating in and supporting me through the early stages of The Dedication Project. Thank you, Chris Warner, for being my sounding board, and listening to my "late night epiphanies". Thank you, Kim Warner, for keeping in touch with all the family members via your infamous Christmas Letters.

Thanks also goes to the Portland State University Art and Social Practice MFA Program: all my peers, faculty, and mentors.